Backyard Bugs

Bzzz, Bzzz!

Mosquitoes in Your Backyard

by Nancy Loewen

illustrated by Rick Peterson

Thanks to our advisers for their expertise, research, knowledge, and advice:

Blake Newton, Extension Entomologist
University of Kentucky

Susan Kesselring, M.A., Literacy Educator
Rosemount–Apple Valley–Eagan (Minnesota) School District

PICTURE WINDOW BOOKS
Minneapolis, Minnesota

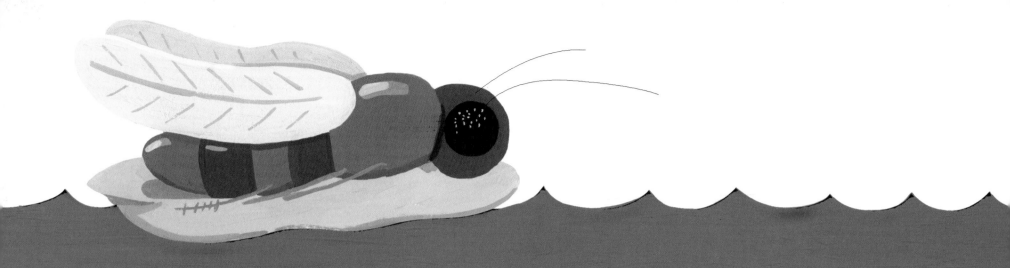

Editorial Director: Carol Jones
Managing Editor: Catherine Neitge
Creative Director: Keith Griffin
Editor: Jill Kalz
Story Consultant: Terry Flaherty
Designer: Nathan Gassman
Page Production: Picture Window Books
The illustrations in this book were created with acrylics.

Picture Window Books
5115 Excelsior Boulevard
Suite 232
Minneapolis, MN 55416
877-845-8392
www.picturewindowbooks.com

Printed in the United States of America.

Library of Congress Cataloging-in-Publication Data
Loewen, Nancy, 1964–
Bzzz, bzzz! : mosquitoes in your backyard / by Nancy Loewen ; illustrated by Rick Peterson.
p. cm. — (Backyard bugs)
Includes index.
ISBN 1-4048-1140-0 (hardcover)
1. Mosquitoes—Juvenile literature. I. Peterson, Rick. II. Title.
QL536.L64 2005
595.77'2—dc22
2005004056

Table of Contents

Don't Bug Me!

Ouch! What's that pinprick you feel on your arm?

Ouch! There's another one on your leg ... and another on your neck!

4

Why are these flying bugs pestering you? They are trying to drink your blood. First, they poke your skin with a long proboscis, or mouthpart. Then, they suck up blood the same way you would drink juice through a straw.

Only female mosquitoes drink blood. They need the proteins in blood to lay their eggs.

The main food for mosquitoes is nectar, a sweet liquid found in flowers.

Uh-oh. Are you starting to feel itchy? The itchiness is caused by the mosquito's saliva. The saliva keeps your blood from thickening so the mosquito can suck it up easily.

8

Mosquitoes don't just drink blood from people. They also like animals, including birds and reptiles.

Female mosquitoes can lay a lot of eggs, even though they mate only once. Females must eat a blood meal before they can lay eggs.

Wanted: Water

Most kinds of mosquitoes lay their eggs on the surface of still water, such as ponds. They may even lay eggs in bird baths and wading pools.

10

Some mosquitoes lay their eggs one at a time, while others group the eggs together like floating rafts.

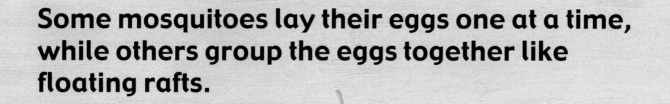

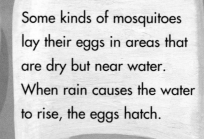

Some kinds of mosquitoes lay their eggs in areas that are dry but near water. When rain causes the water to rise, the eggs hatch.

11

Becoming a Mosquito

Within a couple of days, the eggs hatch. But they aren't mosquitoes yet. They are larvae. They look like little worms with big heads and small hairs growing from their bodies.

The mosquito larvae live just beneath the surface of the water, breathing through tiny tubes. They eat bits of rotting plants. Some kinds of larvae even eat each other!

In cold parts of the world, mosquito eggs that are laid in fall will stay alive all winter. They then hatch in spring.

13

As the mosquito larvae get bigger, they molt, or shed their skin. The fourth time they molt, something changes. They turn into pupae.

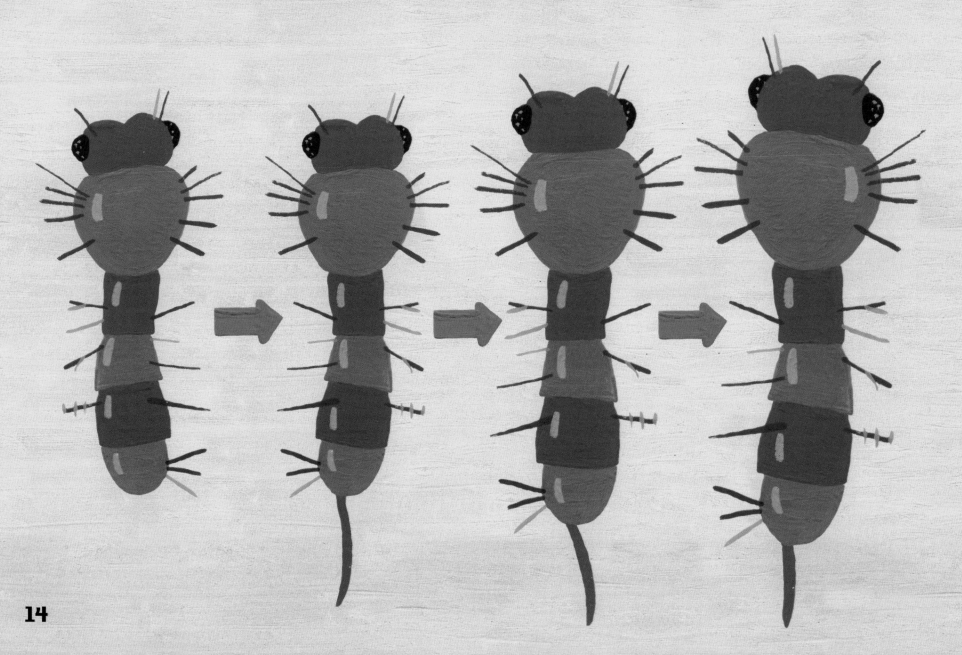

Look over here in this bucket. Do you see those C-shaped creatures? They are mosquito pupae. They have hard outer shells, or cases. Inside the cases, the pupae are becoming adult mosquitoes.

Mosquito pupae float on the water, but they can dive and swim if bothered. They don't eat at all.

Time to Fly

After a few days, the pupa case splits open, and an adult mosquito enters the world. Like a new moth or butterfly, its wings are wet at first. It must let its wings dry and harden before it can fly.

Mosquitoes spend most
of their lives in grass or
bushes. They like damp
areas where their bodies
will not dry out.

Bad Bugs, Good Bugs

Mosquitoes are usually thought of as pests. They make people itchy. They can ruin your outdoor fun. They can also spread deadly diseases, such as malaria and West Nile fever.

Mosquitoes are an important part of nature, however. Birds, bats, frogs, and even other bugs consider mosquitoes a good meal.

Mosquitoes are most active at sunset. They like damp weather with little wind.

No Scratching Allowed

These mosquitoes have made a meal out of you! When you go back inside, be sure to wash the bites with soap and water.

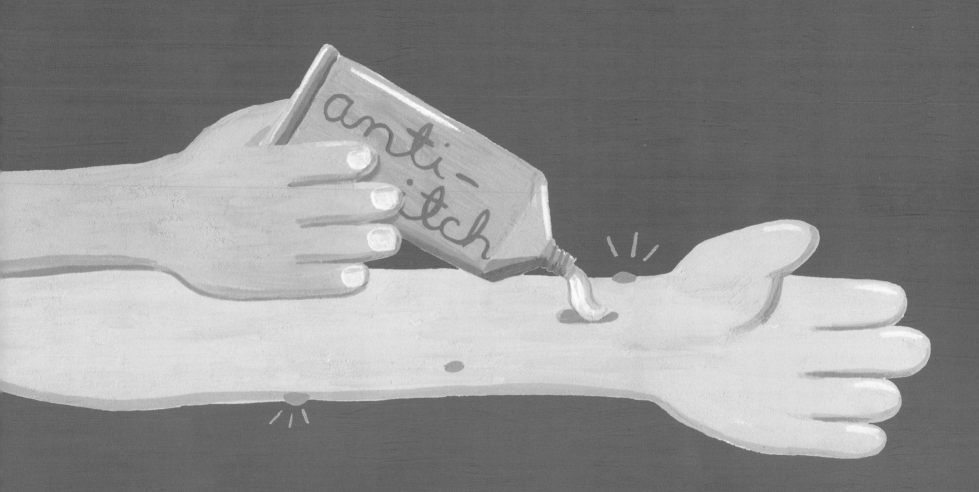

Put on some anti-itch cream, and don't scratch!
If you scratch, the bites will take longer to heal.

Look Closely at a Mosquito

Look at a mosquito through a magnifying glass. How many of these different parts can you see?

- A mosquito uses its **antennae** to touch and smell.

- A mosquito's **eyes** are for seeing its next meal.

- A mosquito sucks blood with its **proboscis**.

- Like all insects, a mosquito has six **legs**.

- A mosquito flaps its **wings** to fly.

head

thorax

abdomen

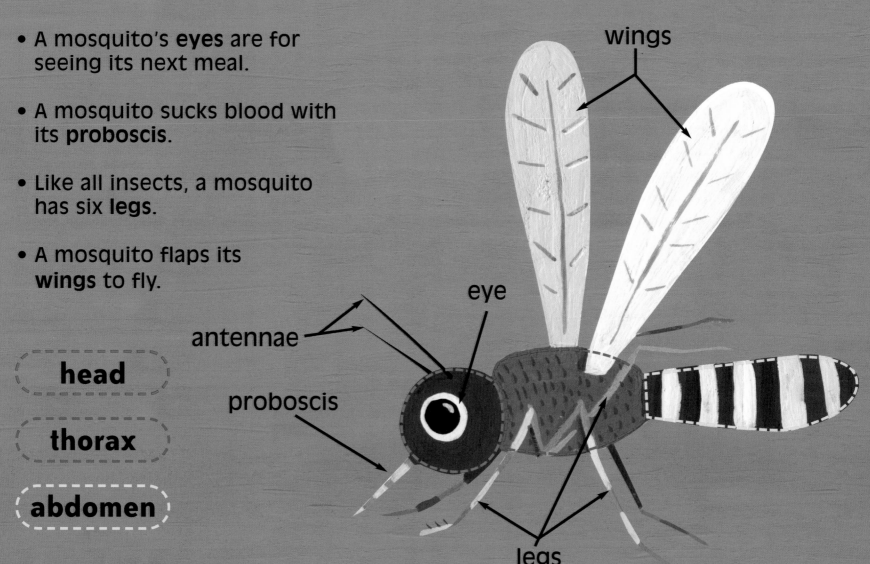

wings

eye

antennae

proboscis

legs

Fun Facts

- Female mosquitoes are attracted to heat, light, bright colors, sweat, and carbon dioxide (the air we breathe out).

- Female mosquitoes make a high-pitched buzzing, whining sound with their wings. It means they're looking for a male.

- Insect repellents contain chemicals that mosquitoes don't like. Repellents come in many forms, including sprays, lotions, candles, and wristbands. Some clothing even has repellent in the fabric.

- To make a simple anti-itching paste, just mix up a little baking soda and water, and rub it over the bites.

Drink Like a Mosquito

Do you want to drink like a mosquito does? Here's how. (And don't worry. There's no blood involved!)

Fill up a small glass with a red drink, such as cranberry juice or fruit punch. Put plastic wrap over the top of the glass. Stretch the plastic wrap so it's really tight.

Get a plastic drinking straw and ask an adult to cut one end at an angle so that it forms a sharp point.

Put the uncut end of the straw in your mouth. You're a mosquito! And you're very thirsty. You spy the glass on the counter—only to you, it's a "blood meal." Poke the straw through the skin (the plastic wrap) and drink up!

Words to Know

larvae – Newly hatched mosquitoes are called larvae (LAR-vee). They look like worms. Larvae is the word for more than one larva.

mate – Male and female mosquitoes mate by joining together special parts of their bodies. After they've mated, the female mosquito can lay eggs.

proboscis – A proboscis (preh-BAH-ses) is a long, hollow mouthpart. A mosquito uses its proboscis to drink blood.

proteins – Proteins are things that are necessary for life. Proteins are found in cells, which are the tiny building blocks that make up all plants and animals.

pupae – When mosquitoes are changing from larvae to adults, they are called pupae (PYOO-pee). Pupae is the word for more than one pupa (PYOO-puh).

saliva – Saliva is another word for spit, or the juices in an animal's mouth.

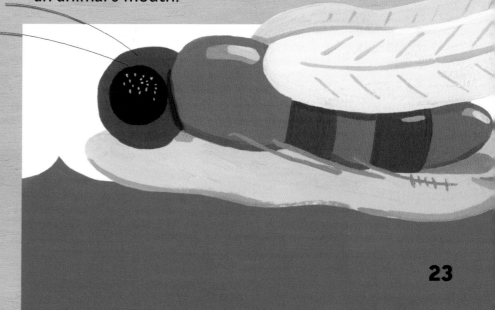

To Learn More

At the Library

Fisher, Enid Broderick. *Mosquitoes*. Milwaukee, Wis.: Gareth Stevens Publications, 1997.

Kalman, Bobbie. *The Life Cycle of a Mosquito*. New York: Crabtree Publishing, 2004.

McDonald, Mary Ann. *Mosquitoes*. Chanhassen, Minn.: Child's World, 2001.

On the Web

FactHound offers a safe, fun way to find Web sites related to this book. All of the sites on FactHound have been researched by our staff. *www.facthound.com*

1. Visit the FactHound home page.
2. Enter a search word related to this book, or type in this special code: 1404811400.
3. Click on the FETCH IT button.

Your trusty FactHound will fetch the best sites for you!

Look for all of the books in the Backyard Bugs series:

Busy Buzzers: *Bees in Your Backyard*

Bzzz, Bzzz! *Mosquitoes in Your Backyard*

Chirp, Chirp! *Crickets in Your Backyard*

Dancing Dragons: *Dragonflies in Your Backyard*

Flying Colors: *Butterflies in Your Backyard*

Garden Wigglers: *Earthworms in Your Backyard*

Hungry Hoppers: *Grasshoppers in Your Backyard*

Living Lights: *Fireflies in Your Backyard*

Night Fliers: *Moths in Your Backyard*

Spotted Beetles: *Ladybugs in Your Backyard*

Tiny Workers: *Ants in Your Backyard*

Weaving Wonders: *Spiders in Your Backyard*

Index